A

MANCHU GRAMMAR,

WITH

ANALYSED TEXTS,

BY

P. G. VON MÖLLENDORFF,

Chinese Customs Service.

SHANGHAI:

PRINTED AT THE AMERICAN PRESBYTERIAN MISSION PRESS.

1892.

G

TABLE OF CONTENTS.

Windham Press is committed to bringing the lost cultural heritage of ages past into the 21st century through high-quality reproductions of original, classic printed works at affordable prices.

This book has been carefully crafted to utilize the original images of antique books rather than error-prone OCR text. This also preserves the work of the original typesetters of these classics, unknown craftsmen who laid out the text, often by hand, of each and every page you will read. Their subtle art involving judgment and interaction with the text is in many ways superior and more human than the mechanical methods utilized today, and gave each book a unique, hand-crafted feel in its text that connected the reader organically to the art of bindery and book-making.

We think these benefits are worth the occasional imperfection resulting from the age of these books at the time of scanning, and their vintage feel provides a connection to the past that goes beyond the mere words of the text.

As bibliophiles, we are always seeking perfection in our work, and so please notify us of any errors in this book by emailing us at corrections@windhampress.com. Our team is motivated to correct errors quickly so future customers are better served. Our mission is to raise the bar of quality for reprinted works by a focus on detail and quality over mass production.

To peruse our catalog of carefully curated classic works, please visit our online store at www.windhampress.com.

INTRODUCTION

THERE is as yet no grammar of the Manchu language in English. WYLIE's translation of the Tsing Wan Ki Mung (清文啟蒙), Shanghai, 1855, a kind of Manchu hand-book for the use of Chinese, though useful and full of interest, is by no means a grammar.

The general interest taken in every language will, of course, be also extended to Manchu; still a few words seem necessary to show the particular usefulness of its study.

There exist in all about 250 works in Manchu, nearly all of which are translations from the Chinese. They consist of translations from the Classics, some historical and metaphysical works, literary essays, collections of famous writers, novels, poetry, laws and regulations, Imperial edicts, dictionaries, phrase books, etc. Most of these translations are excellent, but they are all literal. Executed under the eyes of intelligent princes, they form a reliable expression of the meaning of the Chinese text and have therefore a right to acceptance equal to that enjoyed by commentaries of good writers. Manchu being infinitely easier to learn than Chinese, these translations are a great help towards obtaining a clear insight into Chinese syntax, and scholars like STANISLAS JULIEN, who owed the remarkable precision in his renderings to his knowledge of Manchu, have repeatedly pointed this out. In a letter addressed to Dr. LEGGE he alludes to the study of Manchu as being of great assistance in translating the Classics. Dr. LEGGE, however, in the preface to his translation of the Shuking, pronounced himself against it. The reasons advanced by this great scholar are not very cogent, and, in fact, not knowing the language, he was hardly competent to judge. But, even if he were right, others may be in a different position. Dr. LEGGE was perhaps more fortunate or more gifted than most people and had a thorough mastery of Chinese at the time when ST. JULIEN wrote to him. Those who find Chinese more difficult will be inclined to consider the Manchu translations a great help.

This grammar being intended for the practical purpose of guiding the student in learning to read Manchu works, not of translating into Manchu, everything foreign to the aim is left out, especially all information which properly belongs to the sphere of the dictionary.

SHANGHAI, *February*, 1892.

P. G. VON MÖLLENDORFF.

THE ALPHABET.

	When alone.	In the beginning of a word.	In the middle of a word.	At the end of a word.
a				_see_ n
e				
	when followed by n in the beginning of a word, a space is left to distinguish it from a: [glyph] en [glyph] a			
i				
o				_see_ b
u				
ū				
n	—			like final a, but a vowel preceding shows that it must be n.
k	—	when followed by a, o, ū / " " " e, i, n		
g	—	when followed by a, o, ū / " " " o, i, u		—
h	—	when followed by a, o, ū / " " " e, i, u		—
b	—			the downstroke is longer than that of o.
p	—			
s š	—			
t	—	[glyph] foll. by a, [glyph] foll. by e,	[glyph] ta, [glyph] te, [glyph] after a vowel and before a consonant.	
d	—	[glyph] foll. by a, [glyph] foll. by e,	[glyph] da [glyph] de	
l	—			
m	—			
c	—			
j	—			
y	—			
r	—			
f	—	[glyph] foll. by a or e [glyph] foll by other vowels.	[glyph] foll. by a or e, [glyph] foll. by other vowels	
w	—	[glyph] foll. by a or e	[glyph] foll. by a or e	

For transcribing Chinese syllables:—

k' [glyph], g' [glyph], h' [glyph], ts' [glyph], ts [glyph], dz [glyph], ž [glyph], sy (四) [glyph], c'y (勅) [glyph], jy (智) [glyph]

ng	—	—	[glyph] (a) [glyph] (e)	[glyph]

I. PHONOLOGY.

1. *Alphabet.*

Manchu writing consists of 34 elements, viz., 6 vowels, 18 essentially Manchu consonants and 10 marks specially intended for the rendering of Chinese syllables (*vide* Table).

The 6 vowels are a, e (ä), i, o, u, ū (not ō as generally represented).[1]

The 18 consonants are k, g, h, n, b, p, s, š, t, d, l, m, c, j, y, r, f, w.

The 10 marks are kʻ, gʻ, hʻ, tsʻ, ts, dz, ž, sy, cʻy, jy.[2]

k, g, h, t, d have two forms, one when followed by a, o, ū, the other when followed by e, i, u.

o in the middle or at the end of words may be doubled and then stands for *oo* or *ao*.

If u or ū is followed by a or e, w is placed between them : *juwe* (two) pronounced *jue*.

If a vowel is followed by i, the latter is doubled, except at the end of a word.

No word commences with r, nor with two or more consonants.

t after a vowel and before a consonant, or at the end of a word, is written like *on*.

To distinguish f from w the rule is : at the beginning of a word w occurs only when followed by a or e. F before a and e has an additional stroke at the right.

Manchu is written from top to bottom, the lines following from left to right.[*]

Pronunciation.

Many of the Manchu words are now pronounced with some Chinese peculiarities of pronunciation, so k before i and e=chʻ, g before i and e=ch, h and s before i=hs, etc. H before a, o, u, ū, is the guttural Scotch or German ch.

n is the ordinary sonorous liquid ; only as initial, when followed by iya, iye, iyo, io, it is pronounced like ny : e.g. *niyalma* man=*nyalma* ; *niyengniyeri* spring=*nyingnyiri* ; *niolhon* smooth=*nyolhon* (Radloff, Phonetik, p. 162).

š=sh ; c=ch in Chinese ; j=j in judge ; y when initial=y in yonder.

a, i, o, u, ū as in German.

e=ä, ŏ ; e.g. *ejen* master, Tungusic *äjän* ; *inenggi* day, Tung. *inängî* ; *elgembi* to lead, Tung. *ŏlgöjäm* ; *edun* wind, Tung. *ödyn*.

i=i, y (=Russian ы) ; *hali* meadow=Tung. *kowyr*.

y with an e before and after, is not pronounced : *beye* body=bee (*bĕŏ*). Nor is it heard between i and a, or i and e.

ž=j in *jardin*.

The accent lies always on the last syllable, the same as in Mongolian.

2. *Harmony of Vowels.*

Manchu writing distinguishes 6 vowels ; there are, however, in reality eight, which all occur in stem syllables : a, ä, o, ö, y, i, u, ü. As regards long and short vowels u only has two separate signs.

---

[1] The name of the Emperor 舜 shun is given in Manchu as šŭn.

[2] The y in these 3 Chinese syllables represents the vowel transcribed by Wade with ŭ as in tzŭ and ssŭ, and with ih as in chih and shih.

[*] This alphabet was adopted by the Uigurs from a Syriac or Mandaic source, thence adapted to the Mongolian language and in 1599 slightly altered to suit the pronunciation of Manchu. Unfortunately 3 vowels were left unrepresented : ö, ü, y. By comparing the Tungusic dialects these vowels can be partly restored.

These 8 vowels are divided* into the following groups :—

4 guttural	a	o	y	u
4 palatal	ä	ö	i	ü
4 dental	a	ä	y	i
4 labial	o	u	ö	ü
2 dento-guttural	a		y	
2 labio-guttural	o		u	
2 dento-palatal	ä		i	
2 labio-palatal	ö		ü	
4 wide vowels	a	o	ä	ö) according to the degree of widening or nar-
4 narrow vowels	y	u	i	ü) rowing the inner organs of speech.

The harmony of vowels consists in a certain attraction of vowels physiologically related to each other; in accordance with it a vowel can only be followed by a corresponding one. All the Altaic languages show this peculiarity, the Turkish dialects the most, the Tungusic and Manchu the least. Within stems this harmony of vowels is of interest only to the philologist, but as most of the affixes in Manchu offer the choice between 2 or even 3 vowels (e.g. ha, ho, he; la, le; hon, hun, hūn), a few rules are necessary to show which vowels should be used.

1. Stems terminating in a, e or o, take the same vowel in the affix: *sula-ha* left behind; *mute-re* being able to; *tokto-ho* fixed. Exceptions are given under " Verbs."

For affixes in on, un, ūn (hon, hun, hūn): stems in which a or o occurs twice, or those having i and a, take sometimes ū: *yada-hūn* poor; *šoyos-hūn* folded.

2. Stems of one syllable, terminating in i or u, take mostly e: *bi-he* was; *ku-he* rotten. With one of the affixes on, un, ūn: *his-hūn* bashful.

3. Stems of several syllables terminating in i or u, with a, u, ū, or oo preceding, take mostly a: *mari-ha* returned; *jabu-ha* answered; *tumi-kan* somewhat frequent; *gūni-ha* thought; *kooli-ngga* customary. An exception appears to be: *ashū-re* will refuse. Of affixes in on, un, ūn: *tali-hūn* doubtful; *miosi-hūn* or *hon* wrong.

4. Stems of several syllables terminating in i or u, with e preceding, take e: *julesi-ken* a little forward; *tebu-ngge* laying down; of affixes in on, un, ūn: *wesi-hun* upper; *etu-hun* strong.

5. Stems having u repeated, take mostly e, but sometimes a: *uku-he* accompanied; *ulu-hen* a little wrong; but *usu-kan* a little uncommon.

6. Stems terminating in u with i preceding, take mostly a: *bišu-kan* a little smooth; but also e: *kiru-re* will be in heat.

7. Stems in u and ū, take mostly a: *mukū-ha* breathed in.

8. Stems with two i, take mostly a: *ili-ha* stood; but also e: *iji-re* will weave.

The exceptions for the verbal affixes ha, ra, will be given in extenso under " Verbs."

If two or more affixes are used, the vowel of the first determines the vowels of the others.

The difference between wide and narrow vowels is also used to express the difference of gender, e.g.:—

a male principle (陽 yang).	e female principle (陰 yin).
ama father.	*eme* mother.
amha father-in-law.	*emhe* mother-in-law.
haha man.	*hehe* woman, etc.

---

* I follow J. GRUNZEL, Die Vocalharmonie der Altaischen Sprachen, Sitz. Ber. der Kais. Ak. der Wiss. Wien, 1888, which is based on RADLOFF's eminent work: Phonetik der Nördlichen Türksprachen. Leipzig, 1883.

3. *Diphthongs and Triphthongs.*

In these the rules of vowel harmony are not perceptible :

a may be followed by i, o : ai, ao ; e by i, o : ei, eo ; i by a, e, ii, io, iu ; o by i, o : oi, oo ; u by a, e, i, o : ua, ue, ui, uo ; ū by a, e, i, o : ūa, ūe, ūi, ūo.

Triphthongs are ioa, ioo, io (w) an, io (w) en, ioi, i (y) ao.

Of the above oo stands for ao or ū ; ioo for Chinese yao (要); io(w)an, io(w)en for uan, üen ; ioi for ü ; i(y)oo for iao.

4. *Word-changes and Foreign Words.*

Vowels are often dropped :

a. in the middle of words : *tofohon* fifteen, pronounced *tofhon ; ilha* flower from *ilaha ; utha* hunt—*butaha ; hojhon* son-in-law—*hojihon ; ufhi* part—*ufuhi ; gelhun* fear—*gelehun ; narša* niggard—*naraša ; cirku* pillow—*ciruku* from *cirumbi ; forgon* or *forhon* season—*forohon*, etc.

b. in combination of two words : *ertele* till here—*ere tele, emderi* at the same time—*emu derei ; emuršu* simple—*emu uršu ; erse* such—*ere se ; ergi* this side—*ere gi ; inenggishūn* noon— *inenggi sahūn ; dergi* upper—*dere gi ; baitakū* unemployed—*baita akū ; memema* step-father— *meme ama ; aba* where?—*ai ba ; amargi* behind—*ama ergi, alimbaharakū* inexpressible—*alime baraha akū.*

A final n, not being part of the root, is dropped in combinations : *kumuda* musician— *kumun da ; ilase* three years—*ilan se ; daniyartu* a mythological animal—*daniyan artu*, or transformed in m before b : *dulimba* middle—*dulin ba.*

K and h, g and h sometimes interchange : *emeke—emhe* mother-in-law ; *julge—julehe* formerly.

Foreign words in Manchu are mostly Chinese and Mongol. The latter, like *gobi* desert, *sain* good, have been taken over without change and are difficult to recognize as foreign.

In the beginning of Manchu literature Chinese words were :—

a. borrowed without change, new words for new ideas : ging (京, 經, 更), gung (公, 宮, 功, 工), wang (王), even when an original Manchu word existed : *liyo hūwang* (硫黃 liu huang sulphur) instead of *hurku ; funghūwang* (鳳凰 fêng huang phœnix) instead of *garudai*. It has been calculated that one-third of the Manchu dictionary consists of Chinese words thus borrowed.

b. with slight change in the termination : *ging-gulembi* to honour from 敬 (ching).

c. with an addition explanatory of the meaning : *gin liyan ilha* (金運 chin lien lotus, *ilha* flower) lotus ; *ingturi* or *ingtoro* cherry from 櫻 ying cherry with *turi* bean or *toro* (桃 t'ao) peach.

Other similarities seem to point to more ancient loans : *fi* brush (筆 pi), *fafun* law (法 fa) ; *dulefun* degree (度 tu) ; *kemun* measure (刻 k'e). These may, however, originally spring from the same root (compare e.g. *kemun* with Jakutic *käm* measure).

Manchu words cannot begin with r (Buddhist works contain some transliterated Sanscrit words commencing with r) or ū (*ūlet* is Mongol). They generally terminate in vowels or n. Final r, k and s is only found in onomatopoetic words like *kacar kicir, kafur, kalar kilir*, etc., *cik cak, tok, katak kitik, kas kis*. Words with final m, l, or t, are foreign : *serim* name of a place, *serekul* town in Turkestan, *mandal* Mongol word, a place where sacred rites are practiced, *ūlet* is a Mongol name.

Some few words terminate in b : *tob* right, *cob* mountain peak, *kab kib, cib cab*. The ending ng, if not onomatopoetic as in *ang, cing cang, cung*, etc., shows Chinese origin.

II. ETYMOLOGY.

The words of the Manchu language may be divided into: 1. nouns and adjectives, 2. pronouns, 3. numerals, 4. verbs, 5. adverbs, 6. postpositions, 7. conjunctions, 8. interjections.

1. Nouns and adjectives I treat together, as they have many terminations in common and as many adjectives may be used as nouns and *vice versa*.

The terminations for *nouns* are :—

a. vowels : *abka* heaven, *muke* water, *kesi* favour, *olo* hemp, *huncu* sledge, *boo* house, *buhū* stag.

b. n : *morin* horse, *banin* nature.

c. ka, ko, ku, kū, ho, indicating mostly names of instruments and utensils : *ujika* bow case; *oboko* washing basin ; *hujuku* bellows ; *forikū* drum ; *corho* funnel ; but also *tacikū* school.

d. ha, he, ge, han, hen, gan, gen, gon : *sujaha* tent peg ; *suhe, suhen* commentary, *nedege* news ; *hūsihan* petticoat ; *hūrgan* large net ; *turigen* wages ; *bodogon* intention.

e. ba : *hondoba* whip lash ; *dulimba* middle.

f. bun : *ulabun* tradition.

g. si, ci, cin : *yafasi* gardener ; *aduci* herdsman ; *jacin* second of two brothers.

h. ra, re, ri, ro, rū, ran, ren, ron : *jamaran* quarrel ; *tohoro* circle, wheel ; *heturen* cross beam.

The terminations for nouns *and* adjectives are :—

a. nggi : *inenggi* day ; *etenggi* strong.

b. hiyan, hiyen : *acuhiyan* slander, calumnious.

c. hon, hun, hūn, shun, shūn : *etuhun* power, mighty ; *ijishūn* compliance, compliant.

d. sun : *hūwaliyasun* harmony, peaceful.

e. tu, tun : *iletu* appearance, clear ; *iletun* sign.

f. ki, hi, hin : *jabšaki* luck, lucky ; *hūlhi* stupid ; *aduhi* leather trowsers ; *lekerki, lekerhi, lekerhin* seal.

g. cu, cun : *suilacun* anxiety, anxious.

h. la, lo, le, lan, lon, len : *fangkala* low ; *dorolon* ceremony.

i. ju, ji : *boihoju* terrestrial, spirit of the earth ; *jiduji* quite right ; *boigoji* landlord.

The terminations for *adjectives* are :—

a. ngga, nggo, ngge, nggū : *moringga* riding, *doronggo* regular ; *ambalinggū* (o) earnest.

b. (n) ingge : *niyalmaingge* human.

c. su, da, do, de : *gelesu* timid ; *ubiyada* hated.

d. buru, cuka, cuke : *hataburu, hatacuka* odious ; *ferguwecuke* wonderful.

e. saka : *ekisaka* silent.

Diminutives and augmentatives are formed with the affixes kan, kon, ken, gan, gen, liyan, liyen, cen, si : *ambakan* somewhat large ; *biragan* a small river ; *olhokon* a little dry ; *gelfiyeken* a little pale ; *adaliliyan* somewhat similar ; *ambakaliyan* a little big ; *isheliyen* rather narrow ; *suhecen* a small axe ; *ambakasi* somewhat big.

Adjectives are transformed into nouns by adding *urse* (者) : *tacire urse* (學者) the students, the scholars ; or by adding *ba* (place) : *amba ba* greatness.

The plural of nouns (adjectives remain unchanged) is formed :—

a. by the affixes sa, se, si, so, ta, da, te, ri. These are simply added to the word ; a final n (not being part of the root) is dropped (*hafan—hafasa*) ; but *han* emperor—*hansa*. *Jui* loses final i : *juse* ; *omolo* final lo : *omosi*. Thus *šabi—šabisa* ; *age, agese* ; *aha—ahasi* ; *monggo—monggoso* ; *ama—amata* ; *eme—emete* ; *mafa—mafari*.

Some nouns use several affixes: *urun—urusa* and *uruse; agu—agusa* and *aguse; nakču—nakčusa, nakčuse,* and *nakčuta; gioro* or *gioru—gioroso* and *gioruse; sargan—sargata* and *sargada.*

b. by repeating the noun: *se se* years.

c. by adding numeral terms or words denoting plurality. These are:

Placed *before* the noun: *tanggū* hundred, e.g. *tanggū hala* (百姓) the hundred family names, the people; *tumen* ten thousand (萬), e.g. *tumen jaka* things, all things; *geren* all, e.g. *geren niyalma* all men; the latter is also used in combination with plural forms: *geren ambasa hafasa* the officials.

Placed *after* the noun: *gemu* all, e.g. *bayan gemu* the rich; *tome* all, e.g. *niyalma tome* men, all men; *jergi* rank (等), e.g. *gurgu jergi* the animals; *urse* (者) follows chiefly adjectives or participles, e.g. *bayan urse* the rich; *tacire urse* the scholars, but does not always denote plurality.

Combination of nouns with other affixes: i, ni; de; be; ci.

1. *I, ni. I* is placed after words terminating in a vowel or in n; *ni* follows words terminating in a consonant other than n. After words ending in i (words of Chinese origin excepted) the i may be left out.

This affix denotes:

a. the genitive case or possession, origin, habitation, part, intention with which a thing is done (之), e.g. *boo i ejen* the master of the house; *abkai ejen* the Lord of Heaven, God (天主); *irgen i urse* those of the people; *urgun i doro* the ceremony of congratulation.

b. instrumentality (以), e.g. *suhe i* with an axe.

c. an adverbial expression (然), e.g. *fafun i* legally.

Sometimes the i is left out, e.g. *gūnin sukdun* the spirit of thought, i.e. energy; *siden haha* a supernumerary. The first noun is in such cases employed like an adjective.

Of several nouns dependent on one, only the last of the dependent nouns takes the affix, e.g. *ama jui i boo* the house or houses of the son and of the father. *Ama i jui i boo* means the house of the son of the father.

2. *De* denotes the situation (in, at), the direction (towards, upon, on), the address (to), the remaining with, according to, the locative and the dative: *gurun de* in the empire, towards the empire; *hoton de* in or to the town; *doron de* according to custom, solemnly; *na de* on earth; *ere niyalma de bumbi* to give to this (*ere*) man (*niyalma*); *tere niyalma de henduhe* he spoke with that man; *dere de sindambi* to place on the table; *si aibide genembi* where (*aibide*) are you (*si*) going to? *tuware de ja gojime yabure de mangga* though (*gojime*) easy (*ja*) to look at (*tuware de*), it is difficult (*mangga*) to perform (*yabure de*); *niyalma de* it is for man to; *abka de* it is for heaven to (*hominis est, cœli est*); *juwe de gemu sartabure de isinambi* to come to (*isinambi*) delaying (*sartabure de*) altogether (*gemu*) in either (*juwe de*) 兩下裡都至於就擱; *gemu* like the Chinese 都 *tu* is here expletive.

3. *Be* denotes the direct complement of the verb, the accusative, e.g. *baita be gaimbi* to take a thing; *erdemui beyebe dasambi* by virtue we cultivate the body (*beye be* ourselves). *Be* is sometimes used as an expletive, e.g. *hūwašabukū mutebukū tacikū tacihiyakū be ilibufi tacibume. hūwašabukū serengge ujire be tacihiyakū serengge tacibure be mutebukū serengge gabtabure be,* establish (*ilibufi*) colleges, academies, schools and gymnasia for the instruction (*tacibume*) *of the people.* A college is for nourishment, an academy (and a school) for instruction, a gymnasium for archery (Mencius, Gabelentz p. 90, Legge p. 118). This use of *be* might be explained as an *ellipsis,* a verb like to give (*bumbi*) or to teach (*tacimbi*) being understood. It may be left out, if the sentence is otherwise clear, e.g. *bithe arambi* to write a letter.

4. *Ci* is the sign of the ablative case (from, out of), denotes separation and is used in comparisons, e.g. *ereci amasi* henceforward ; *daci dubede isitala* from beginning to end ; *ubaci goro akū* not far from this ; *ama eniye ci fakcafi, booci aljafi ineŋgi goidaha* taking leave of his father and mother, he was long separated from his family ; *yaci neneme jihe bihe* which came first ?

It serves to form the comparative, e.g. *minci amba* bigger than myself.

2. PRONOUNS.

a. Personal Pronouns.

bi I, *si* thou, *i* he (*tere* that), *be* we, *muse* we, *suwe* you, *ce* they. *Muse* means (like the Pekingese 咱 們 tsa men) we that are speaking together, we that belong to one family, one clan, one nation. The above are declined as follows :—

nom.	*bi* I	*be* we	*muse* we	*si* thou	*suwe* you	*i* he, she, it	*ce* they
gen.	*mini*	*meni*	*musei*	*sini*	*suweni*	*ini*	*ceni*
dat.	*minde*	*mende*	*musede*	*sinde*	*suwende*	*inde*	*cende*
acc.	*mimbe*	*membe*	*musebe*	*simbe*	*suwembe*	*imbe*	*cembe*
abl.	*minci*	*menci*	*museci*	*sinci*	*suwenci*	*inci*	*cenci.*

For I, myself, etc., *beye* is added to the genitive : *mini beye, sini beye,* etc. For he himself *ini beye* or *gūla beye* is used.

b. Possessive Pronouns. These are formed by adding *ngge* to the genitive of the personal pronouns : *miningge* mine, *siningge* thine, etc. Often the genitive without *ngge* is thus employed : *meni morin* our horse. *Ere* this, *tere* that frequently stand for the third person : *terei gūnin* his opinion ; *eseingge* theirs, belonging to them.

c. Demonstrative Pronouns. These are *ere* this, *tere* that :—

nom.	*ere* this	*ese* these	*tere* that	*tese* those
gen.	*erei, ereni*	*esei*	*terei*	*tesei*
dat.	*ede, erede*	*esede*	*tede, terede*	*tesede*
acc.	*erebe*	*esebe*	*terebe*	*tesebe*
abl.	*ereci*	*eseci*	*tereci*	*teseci.*

If used as adjectives, *ere* and *tere* do not add the case affixes. Sometimes *uba* this and *tuba* that are used, but always alone, not in combination with nouns.

d. Interrogative Pronouns. These are *we* (gen. *wei*, dat. *wede*, acc. *webe*, abl. *weci*) who ? *ai* (acc. *aimbe*, abl. *ainci*) what ? which ? *ya* who ? what ? With *we* are formed *weingge, weike* which ? of what nature ? With *ai : aibi, ai gese, aiba* what ? *ai yadare* how much ? *aba* where ? etc. With *ya : yaci* who ? what ? *yaka* how ?

At the end of interrogative sentences it is common to append ni or o, e.g. *marimbio* shall I back out ? When following the future participle in ra (re, ro) o sometimes implies a request : *minde hūlabureo* do cause me to study ! (*hūlambi* to study, *hūlabumbi* passive or causative, *hūlabure* future participle).

e. Indefinite Pronouns : *aika, aimaka* somebody, *ya* everybody, *yamaka* whoever, etc.

3. NUMERALS.

a. The Cardinal Numerals are :—

1	*emu, emke*	6	*ninggun*
2	*juwe*	7	*nadan*
3	*ilan*	8	*jakūn*
4	*duin*	9	*uyun*
5	*sunja*	10	*juwan*

11	*juwan emu*	70	*nadanju*
12	„ *juwe*	80	*jakūnju*
13	„ *ilan*	90	*uyunju*
14	„ *duin*	100	*tanggū*
15	*tofohon*	101	*tanggū emu*
16	*juwan ninggun*, etc.	200	*juwe tanggū*
20	*orin*	300	*ilan tanggū*, etc.
21	*orin emu*, etc.	1000	*minggan*
30	*g sin*	10,000	*tumen*
40	*dehi*	100,000	*juwan tumen*
50	*susai*	1,000,000	*tanggū tumen.*
60	*ninju*		

The higher numerals (up to 100 trillions *buju baja*) are not originally Manchu, but were introduced into Buddhist works in imitation of Tibetan numerals which again were originally Sanscrit.

b. The Ordinal Numerals are formed by adding *ci* to the cardinals, dropping a final n except in *juwan* ten and *tumen* ten thousand, in which two the n is part of the root:

The first *uju, ujui, ujuci, tuktan, cmuci,* the very first *ujui uju, niongnio, bonggo.*

The second *jai, jaici, juweci.*

The third *ilaci*	The ninth *uyuci*
The fourth *duici*	The tenth *juwanci*
The fifth *sunjaci*	The eleventh *juwan emuci*
The sixth *ningguci*	The hundredth *tanggūci*
The seventh *nadaci*	The thousandth *minggaci*
The eighth *jakūci*	The ten thousandth *tumenci.*

For the days of the month and for the months and years other expressions are in use: the first day of the month *ice*; the first month *tob biya* (正 月); the first year (of an emperor's reign) *sucungga aniya* (元 年); the 3rd day of the 3rd moon *ilangga inenggi*; the 7th day of the 7th moon *nadangga inenggi*; the 16th day of the 1st moon *niohun*; the 11th moon *omšon biya*; the 12th moon *jorgon biya.*

The first of 2 or 3 sons is *uda*, the second *jacin.*

d. Distributive Numerals are formed by adding *ta, te, to,* to the cardinals, final n being dropped as with the ordinal numerals (except in *juwan* 10 and *tumen* 10,000).

one by one *emte* (for *emute*)	by	8 *jakūta*	by	50 *susaita.*
by twos *juwete*	„	9 *uyute*	„	60 *ninjute.*
„ threes *itata*	„	10 *juwanta*	„	70 *nadanjuta* (*te*).
„ fours *duite*	„	15 *tofohoto*	„	80 *jakūnjute.*
„ fives *sunjata*	„	20 *orita*	„	90 *uyunjute.*
„ sixes *ninggute*	„	30 *gūsita*	„	100 *tanggūta.*
„ sevens *nadata*	„	40 *dehite*	„	1000 *minggata.*
			„	10,000 *tumente.*
			„	several *udute.*

e. Fractional numerals: *dulin, dulga, andala, tubi, dulimba, hontoho* half; $\frac{1}{4}$ *duin ci emu*; $\frac{1}{3}$ *ilan ci emu.*

f. Multiplicative Numerals are formed by adding *ubu* or *rsu* (*ursu*) to the cardinals with elision of final n (except as above in *juwan* and *tumen*):

single *emursu, emu ubu*;

double *jursu, juwe ubu, ubui*; *ubui fulu* (twice as much), *juru, bakcin*;

8

threefold *ilarsu ilan ubu ;*

ninefold *uyursu ;*

hundredfold *tanggūrsu.*

With reference to textile fabrics *ri* is used : *ilari* threefold, *sunjari* fivefold, *jakūri* eightfold.

Other numeral expressions are : *gemu* both, *durbejengge* square, with four angles.

4. VERBS.

There are in Manchu pure verbal stems of one and more syllables like *o* to be, *ara* to write, and verbs derived from nouns and adjectives.

The more common syllables used in case of such derivation are:

ta, to, te, da, do, de : *gosin* humanity—*gositambi* (also without any insertion : *gosi—mbi*); *jali* crafty—*jalidambi* to cheat.

na, no, ne : *abdaha* a leaf—*abdahanambi* to leaf ; *acan* union—*acanambi* to meet.

la, le : *hiyoošun* (孝順) filial piety—*hiyoošulambi* to treat with filial piety ; *aba* a hunt—*abalambi* to hunt.

du, ndu : *hiyoošun* filial piety—*hiyoošundumbi.*

ra, ro, re : *gisun* word—*gisurembi* to speak.

ša, šo, še : *injeku* merry—*injekušembi* to laugh at ; *adali* similar—*adališambi* to be similar.

In some cases it is doubtful whether the verb is derived from the noun or whether the latter is of verbal derivation : *isan* a meeting, *isambi* to meet ; *iren* the track of fish, *irenembi* to ruffle the water (as fish do).

There are further syllables which, when added to the stem of verbs form new verbs. These are :

ja, mostly reflexive : *gūninambi* to think, *gūninjambi* the same ; *isambi* to meet, *isamjambi* to collect.

nu, ndu, mostly cooperative : *injembi* to laugh, *injendumbi* to laugh together (*injenumbi*); *arambi* to do, *arandumbi* to do together.

ca, co, ce, cooperative and frequentative : *injembi* to laugh, *injecembi* to laugh together ; *dedumbi* to sleep, *deducembi* to sleep together.

ji : *wambi* to kill, *wajimbi* to die ; *arambi* to do, *aranjimbi* to come to do.

na, no, ne : *isimbi* to come near, *isinambi* to arrive.

An accumulation of these syllables frequently occurs : *ijumbi—ijurambi—ijuršambi* to besmear ; *abalambi* to hunt, *abalanambi* to go hunting, *abalanjimbi* to come to the hunt, *abalandumbi* to hunt together; *acambi* to meet, *acalambi* to agree upon, *acamjambi* to collect, *acanambi* to meet, *acandumbi* to meet together, *acanjimbi* to come to meet.

Moods and Tenses. To express the moods and tenses the Manchu verb has 23 forms.

1. The stem ; the moods and tenses are produced by adding the following affixes to the stem of the verb :—

2. *mbi*, 3. *me*, 4. *ha* (*he, ho, ka, ke, ko, ngka, ngke, ngko*), 5. *ra* (*re, ro, ndara, ndere*), 6. *ci*, 7. *ki*, 8. *fi* (*pi, mpi*), 9. *mbihe*, 10. *habi* (*hebi, hobi, kabi, kebi, kobi*), 11. *habihe* (*hebihe, hobihe, kabihe, kebihe, kobihe*), 12. *habici* (*hebici, hobici, kabici, kebici, kobici*); 13. *cibe*, 14. *cina* (*cun*), 15. *kini*, 16. *mbime*, 17. *mbifi*, 18. *nggala* (*nggele, nggolo*), 19. *mbumbi*, 20. *mbubumbi*, 21. *ngge*, 22. *le* (*lengge*), 23. *leme* (*lame*).*

---

* Whenever hereafter any of these affixes is referred to, its number as here given will be quoted in brackets.

Of these *ha* (4), *ra* (5), *habi* (10), *habihe* (11), *habici* (12), and *nggala* (18) are subjected to the laws of vowel harmony.

Taking in order the parts of the paradigm *arambi* to write I will now explain each form.

1. The stem is *ara* which at the same time serves as the Imperative: *ara* write !

2. By adding *mbi* we obtain the Present Tense: *ara—mbi* I write (there being no distinction of persons, this stands for I, thou, he, we, you, they write).

3. *Me* added to the stem makes the Infinitive: *ara—me* to write ; this form is also an Indefinite Gerund : writing.

4. The affix *ha* forms the preterite : *ara—ha* I wrote. It is also a past participle : written, having written.

5. The affix *ra* forms the Future : *ara—ra* I shall write ; it is also a participle : writing, going to write.

6. *Ci* makes a Conditional Tense : *ara—ci* I should write, if I wrote, should I write, sometimes to be translated by the present tense implying a doubt.

7. *Ki* forms a Subjunctive of the present : *ara—ki* may he write.

8. *Fi* forms a past Gerund : *ara—fi* having written, after having written.

The above eight are the fundamental forms ; the 15 others are formed by adding affixes to them. Those which are added to the stem are :—

9. *Mbihe* forming an Imperfect Tense : *ara—mbihe* I was writing.

10. *Habi* forming an Indefinite Past : *ara—habi* I have written.

11. *Habihe* forming a Pluperfect : *ara—habihe* I had written.

12. *Habici* forming a Past Conditional Tense : *ara—habici* if I had written.

13. *Cibe* forming an Adversative : *ara—cibe* although I may write, even if I write.

14. *Cina* forming a Concessive : *ara—cina* may he write if he likes, may he write what he likes. An old form *cun* (*ara—cun*) is found in a translation of the Shiking (Book of Odes).

15. *Kini* forming an Optative : *ara—kini* would that he wrote ! *Cina* and *kini* are also used in an imperative or passive sense.

16. *Mbime* forming a Gerund : *ara—mbime* whilst writing.

17. *Mbifi* forming a Gerund : *ara—mbifi* having written.

18. *Nggala* denotes that a thing has not yet been done : *ara—nggala* before I wrote, before writing.

19. *Mbumbi* forming the Passive or Causative Mood : *ara—mbumbi* is written, causes to write. This then becomes a new verb, which as an independent stem (*arambu*) takes all the other affixes.

20. *Mbubumbi* forming a Causative of the Passive : *ara—mbubumbi* causes to be written.

The following affixes are added to the forms in *ha* (4) and *ra* (5) :—

21. *Ngge* forming Verbal Nouns and Adjectives : *ara—ha—ngge*, *ara—ra—ngge* that which is written, the writing ; that which he has written ; he is writing ; he who is writing.

22. *Le* adds an indefinite meaning : *ara—ha—le*, *ara—ra—le* whoever writes, whatever is written. This affix is originally *ele* (whoever) and the Chinese-Manchu Grammar Tsing Wen Ki Mung (vol. II, fol. 32 *b*) is wrong in giving two forms *le* and *la*, subjecting them to the law of harmony. This form also takes the affix *ngge*: *ara—ha—le—ngge*, *ara—ra—le—ngge*—whosoever is writing.

23. *lame* (*leme*) added to the future in *ra* (5) renders the meaning adverbial : *ara—ra—lame* in the manner of writing.

PARADIGM OF *ARAMBI* TO WRITE.

1. Imperative	*ara*	write!
2. Present Tense	*arambi*	I write.
3. Infinitive	*arame*	to write.
4. Preterite	*araha*	I wrote.
5. Future	*arara*	I shall write.
6. Conditional	*araci*	should I write.
7. Subjunctive Present	*araki*	may he write.
8. Past Gerund	*arafi*	having written.
9. Imperfect	*arambihe*	I was writing.
10. Indefinite Past	*arahabi*	I have written.
11. Pluperfect	*arahabihe*	I had written.
12. Past Conditional	*arahabici*	if I had written.
13. Adversative	*aracibe*	although he may write.
14. Concessive	*aracina*	may he write.
15. Optative	*arakini*	would that he wrote.
16. Gerund I.	*arambime*	whilst writing.
17. „ II.	*arambifi*	having written.
18. „ III.	*aranggala*	before writing.
19. Passive	*arambumbi*	it is written.
20. Causative or Passive	*arambubumbi*	I cause to be written.
21. Verbal Noun	*arahangge, ararangge*	the writing, the writer.
22. Indefinite	*arahale, ararale*	whoever writes.
23. Adverbial	*araralame*	in the manner of writing.

IRREGULARITIES.

1. The following verbs have an irregular Imperative :—

baimbi	to request	—*baisu.*
bimbi	to be	—*bisu.*
gaimbi	to receive	—*gaisu.*
jembi	to eat	—*jefu.*
jimbi	to come	—*jio, ju.*
ombi	to become	—*oso.*
tucimbi	to go forth	—*tusinu.*
wasimbi	to fall	—*wasinu.*
wesimbi	to rise	—*wesinu.*

2. The sign of the Past Tense *ha, he, ho, ka, ke, ko, ngka, ngke, ngko;* and the sign of the Future *ra, re, ro, ndara, ndere, ndoro* are subject to the laws of vowel harmony. The general rules are :—

a. verbs with the stem in *a* have *ha (ka)* and *ra.* Exceptions with *ha, re: buktalambi, cihalšambi, cilcilambi, maimašambi, manjurambi, miyoocalambi, nionggalambi, niyakurambi, tungnigambi.* With *he, ra: derakulambi, faishalambi, sosambi.* With *ho, ro: morilambi.*

b. verbs with the stem in *e* have *he (ke)* and *re.* Exceptions: *siderilembi (ha, re); giyoloršembi (ho, ro).*

c. verbs with the stem in *o* have *ho (ko)* and *ro.* Exceptions : *doombi (ha, re); fombi (ha, re); gombi, goha, gondoro; joombi (ha, re); leombi* or *loombi (ha, re); neombi (he, re); niyaniombi (ha, re); šombi (ha, re); tungniombi (ha, re); yombi, yoha, yoro, yondoro.*

d. verbs in n with *a* preceding have *ha* (*ka*), *ra* (*re*). Exception : *niyanggumbi* (*he, re*).

e. verbs in i with *a* preceding have *ha* (*ka*), *ra* (*re*). Exception : *alanggimbi* (*he, re*).

f. verbs in i with *e* preceding have *he* (*ke*), *re*. Exception : *kesimbi* (*ha, re*).

g. verbs in n with *e* preceding have *he* (*ke*), *re*. Exception : *feksimbi* (*ha, re*).

Dahambi forms *daha* (instead of *dahaha*), *bahambi* forms *baha*.

A number of verbs, however, contrary to the above rules, take *ha, ra; ha, re; he re; ho, ro; ka, ra; ka, re; ke, re; ko, ro; ha* and *ka, ra; ha* and *ka, re; ha* and *ke, re; ha* and *he, re; ha* and *ho, ro; he* and *ho, ro; he* and *ke, re; ho* and *ko, ro; ke* and *ko, ro*. It would be to no purpose to give the long lists of these verbs, Sakharoff's Dictionary gives the affixes used by each verb.

The following verbs are only used in the Indefinite Past: *abulikabi, absakabi, bemberekebi, delerekebi, farakabi, feherekebi, geigerekebi, genggerekebi, giyabsarakabi, gūwasakabi, ilmerekebi, jakjarakabi, jerekebi, joholikabi, juyekebi, laifarakabi, lebderekebi, lukdurekebi, werukebi.*

The following verbs are found only as participles in *ka, ke* and *ko: fuseke, niyekseke, oyoko, sureke, uldeke, undarako.*

Certain verbs form the Preterite in *ngka, ngke, ngko*, the future in *ndara, ndere, ndoro*. Others form the Past Gerund in *pi, mpi* instead of in *fi*. The following list gives the verbs with these irregularities, including the verbs already mentioned with irregular Imperatives.

LIST OF IRREGULAR VERBS.

Verb.	Imperative.	Preterite.	Future.	Past Gerund.
bahambi		baha		
baimbi	baisu	baiha	baire	
bambi		bangka	bandara	
bimbi	bisu	bihe	bisire	
bisarambi				bisarapi
bombi		bongko	bore, bondoro	infin. bonme
cambi		caha, cangka	cara	cafi
colgorombi		colgoroko	colgororo	colgoropi
dahambi		daha		
deserembi				deserepi
duksembi				duksepi
dulembi				dulepi
eldembi		eldeke	eldere	eldepi
eyembi				eyepi
falarambi				falarapi
farambi		faraha, faraka	farara	farapi
febumbi (fembi)		febuhe	febure	fempi
fombi		foha	fore	fompi, condit. fomci
fosombi				fosopi
fumbi		fungke		fumpi
gaimbi	gaisu	gaiha	gaire	
gajimbi	gaju			
gerembi		gerehe, gereke	gerere, gerendere	
gombi		goha	gondoro	
guwembi		guwengke	guwendere	guwempi, cond. guwenci
gūmbi		gūha	gūndere	
gūwaliyambi (hū)		gūwaliyaka	gūwaliyara	gūwaliyapi, hūwaliyapi

Verb.	Imperative.	Preterite.	Future.	Past Gerund.
hafumbi		hafuka	hafundere	hafupi
hatambi		hataha	hatara, hatandara	
jailambi		jailaha	jailara, jailandara	
jaksambi				jaksapi
jalambi		jalaka	jalara, jalandara	jalapi
jalumbi		jaluka	jalura	jalupi
jembi	jefu	jeke, jengke	jetere, jendere	jempi
jimbi	jio, ju	jihe	jidere	[jongki
jombi		jongko	jondoro	jompi, cond. jonci, opt.
jumbi		jungke	jure	jumpi, opt. jubki
jurambi				jurapi
juwambi		juwangka, juwaka	juwara, jore	juwampi
niorombi				nioropi
ombi, oombi	oso	oho	ojoro	
sambi		sangka	sara	sampi
sembi		sengke	sere	
sosombi		sosoko	sosoro	sosopi
sumbi		sungke, suhe	sure	
šahūrambi		šahūraka	šahūrara	šahūrapi
šambi		šangka, šaha	šara	
šarambi				šarapi
šumbi		šungke	šure	šumpi
teyembi		teyehe	teyere, teyendere	
tucimbi	tucinu	tucihe, tucike	tucire	
ukambi		ukaha, ukaka	ukara, ukandara	
wasimbi	wasinu	wasika, ha	wasire	
wembi		wengke	were, wendere	wempi, inf. weme
wesimbi	wesinu	wesike	wesire	wesipi
yombi		yoha	yoro, yondoro	
yumbi		yungke	yudere, yundere	yumpi

The Verb in the Negative.

Negation is expressed by *akū* not, is not (無, 不, 未, 沒 有), *waka* not, no (不 是), *ume* (莫) do not, *unde* not yet, *umai* not, not at all.

When joined to the Present Tense *akū* simply follows: *bi gisurembi akū* I do not speak. With other verbal forms *akū* loses its *a*: *araha—kū* he has not written, *genehe—kū* he did not go. Joined to the Future the *a* of *akū* remains: *arar—akū* he will not write, *gener—akū* he will not go. The affixes *ci*, *fi*, and *ngge* follow *akū*: *generakūci* if he does not go, *akūfi* not existing, *bisirakūngge* those who are not present (不 在 的). When alone *akū* takes the regular affixes: *bi akūmbi* I am not. A double negation often occurs, *akūngge akū* (無 不): *serakūngge akū* nothing unsaid, he says everything.

In interrogative sentences *akū* adds an *n*: *si sembio akūn* will you eat or not?

Waka not, no, is either employed like *akū*, but without taking the affixes, or stands at the beginning of a sentence and then means no: *manju bithe hūlambi wakao* do you not study Manchu?

Ume followed by the verb in the Future Tense (*ra*) expresses prohibition: *ume fusihūšara* do not despise; *ume gunire* do not think.

Unde is preceded by the verb in the Future Tense (*ra*): *bi sabure unde* I have not yet seen.

5. ADVERBS.

Manchu Adverbs are either primitive or derived from nouns, pronouns, numerals, or verbs.

a. Primitive Adverbs are indeclinable words like *inu* yes, *coro* after to-morrow, etc., of which there are a great number.

b. Nouns are transformed into Adverbs by the affix *i*: *an-i* according to custom; *de: doron de* solemnly; *ci: daci* from the beginning, naturally; *dari: biyadari* monthly. Many adjectives, especially those ending in *saka, cuka, cuke* may be used as Adverbs.

c. The Pronouns furnish a great number of Adverbs: *aide* where?, *aibaci* wherefrom?, etc.

d. Most of the Numerals may be used as Adverbs. To the Ordinal Numerals *de* is added: *jaide* secondly. Others are formed by adding *geri, nggeri, jergi, mudan, mari: emgeri* once; *ilanggeri* thrice; *emu mudan, emu mari* once. *Leme* forms multiplicative Adverbs: *tumenleme* 10,000 fold.

e. The verbal forms in *me (arame), mbime (arambime), leme, lame* preceded by the verb in the Future Tense (*araralame*) may all be used as adverbial expressions.

f. Many Adverbs are formed by adding the negation *akū: erin akū* never; *hercun akū* unexpectedly.

6. POSTPOSITIONS.

These are either simple or compound.

a. The Simple Postpositions are the case affixes *i, de, ci: i* with, with the help of: *suhe i* with the axe; *de* in, at, on, towards, upon, to: *hoton de* in or to the town; *ci* from, out of: *boo ci* from the house.

b. The Compound Postpositions follow the noun without any case affix or are preceded by *i, de, be,* or *ci: omoi jakade* near the pond; *alin de isitala* as far as to the mountain; *fafun be dahame* in accordance with the law; *julge ci ebsi* from antiquity.

7. CONJUNCTIONS.

Beside several postpositions being used as Conjunctions like *jakade* when, because, *isitala* as soon as, *turgunde* as, because, etc., there are primitive Conjunctions like *uthai* therefore, *damu* but, and derivatives of verbs like *cohome* consequently, *tuwame* with regard to, *oci* (from *ombi*) if, *ocibe* although, *ofi* because, of nouns like *fonde* at the time when, *bade* when, of pronouns like *aibe......aibe* as well as, and of numerals like *emgeri......emgeri* now... ..now.

8. INTERJECTIONS.

There is a great variety of Interjections in Manchu: *ai* ah, *ara* alas, *yaka* ah, *adada* bravo, *cibse* hush, *takasu* stop, *cu* off, etc. A number of onomatopoetic interjections are used as verbs when followed by *sembi* (to speak): *kab* snap, *kab sembi* to snap at; *kanggūr kinggur* helter-skelter, with *sembi* to fall with a great noise.

III. SYNTAX.

The position of words in a sentence is governed by the general rule, that every word precedes that by which it is governed. Thus the genitive stands before the noun on which it depends, e.g. *boo i ejen* the master of the house.

The adjective, participle, or demonstrative pronoun precedes its noun, e.g. *nikan mudan* the Chinese pronunciation; *mutere baita* a thing which can be done; *tere niyalma* that man.

The object stands before its governing verb, e.g. *bithe arambi* I write a letter.

The verb stands last in the sentence and can only be followed by a conjunction. The sentence "when 1 had given that thing to my father yesterday" would be rendered in Manchu: *sikse* (yesterday) *bi* (I) *mini ama de* (to my father) *tere* (that) *baita be* (thing) *buhabihe* (pluperfect of *bumbi* to give) *manggi* (when).

Subordinate verbs precede the conclusive verb and take the form of the Past Gerund in *fi* or the Conditional in *ci*, e.g. *cooha be gaifi amasi bederehe* he took (*gaifi*, Past Gerund of *gaimbi*) the army (*cooha be*) and retreated (*bederehe*, Preterit of *bederembi*) backwards (*amasi*); having collected his army he retreated.

Coordinate verbs standing first in the same sentence take the form of the Infinitive (or Gerund) in *me* and only the last verb takes the tense affix required, e.g. *muse niyalma jalan de banjifi inenggidari jaboŝome seoleme, beye dubentele kiceme faŝŝame dulekengge be amcame¦ aliyara gosihon babi*, we men (*muse niyalma*) having been born (*banjifi*, Past Gerund of *banjimbi*) into the world (*jalan de*), are daily (*inenggidari*) afflicted (*joboŝome*, Gerund of *joboŝombi*) and vexed (*seoleme*, Gerund of *seolembi*), till the end (*dubentele*) we fatigue (*kiceme*, Gerund of *kicembi*) and exert (*faŝŝame*, Gerund of *faŝŝambi*) ourselves (*beye*), expecting (*aliyara*, Future Participle of *aliyambi*) again and again (*amcame*) that which is past (*dulekengge be*) we are really (*babi*) miserable (*gosihon*).

The following pages will serve as reading lessons and as exercises for the elucidation of Manchu syntax. The text is taken from the "*Tanggū meyen*" (Hundred Chapters) a book of Manchu-Chinese dialogues, v. page 10 of my "Essay on Manchu Literature" in Journal of C. B. of R. A. S. vol. xxiv (1890). The Chinese version of these dialogues is familiar to every student of Chinese, as it forms the "Hundred Lessons" in the Tzŭ-êrh-chi of Sir Thomas Wade, of whose classical English translation I have availed myself. By comparing the Chinese of these dialogues the interesting fact will be noticed that certain peculiarities of Pekingese are Manchuisms foreign to ordinary "Mandarin."

1	2	3	4
(Manchu script)	(Manchu script)	(Manchu script)	(Manchu script)

SENIOR. So I hear you are studying Manchu, eh? that's right. Manchu is with us Manchus the first and foremost of essentials; it is to us, in short, what the language spoken in his own part of the country is to a Chinese; so it would never do to be without a knowledge of Manchu, would it?

donjici, Condit. tense (6) of *donjimbi* to hear: I hear, but I am not sure, whether it is so

si thou

te now

manju Manchu

bithe book

tacimbi Present Tense (2) to learn

sembi (2) to say, here merely closing the report he heard

umesi very

sain good

manju Manchu

gisun word, speech

serengge Future Part. of *sembi* to say, namely

musei we, with genitive affix *i*, of us

manjusai Manchus, gen. plur. *sa-i*

ujui first, with genitive affix *i* ⎫ the first of
uju first ⎭ the first

oyonggo important

baita thing, matter

uthai therefore, it is as

nikasai, pl. of *nikan* Chinese (*nikasa*) with gen. affix *i* of the Chinese

meni meni every

ba place

i genitive affix

gisun word, speech

i genitive affix

adali alike, similar to

bahanarakūci Fut. (5) of *bahanambi* to comprehend, with negation *akū* and *oci* Conditional (6) of *ombi* to be, if you should not know

ombio Pres. Tense (2) of *ombi* to be, with interrogative *o*, will that do?

1	2	3	4

JUNIOR. To be sure not. I have been studying Chinese for over ten years, but I am still as far as ever from seeing my way in it. Then if I can't master Manju and learn to translate, I shall have broken down at both ends of the line.

inu yes, indeed

waka not

oci Cond. (6) of *ombi* to be, it may

ai what?

bi I

juwan ten

aniya year

funceme Inf. (3) of *funcembi* to exceed, coordinate definite verb followed by *taciha*: I have exceeded and learned

nikan Chinese

bithe book

taciha Pret. (4) of *tacimbi* to learn: I have learned

tetele from *te* now and *tele* till; up to the present, still

umai not at all

dube point, end, extreme

da beginning, *dube da* the very beginning

tuciraku̅ Fut. (5) of *tucimbi* to appear, with *aku̅* not: it does not appear

jai second, further

aikabade if

manju Manchu

bithe book

hūlaraku̅ Fut. (5) of *hūlambi* to read, to study, with *aku̅* not: shall not study

ubaliyambure Fut. partic. (5) of *ubaliyambumbi* to translate

be accusative affix

taciraku̅ Fut. (5) of *tacimbi* to learn with *aku̅* not

oci Cond. (6) of *ombi* to be

juwe de two, with postpos. in

gemu both, alike

sartabure Fut. (5) of *sartabumbi* to be delayed

de postpos. to

isinambi to arrive

1	2	3	4

uttu thus

ofi Past Gerund (8) of *ombi* to be: having been

emude firstly

oci Cond. (6) of *ombi* to be

age elder brother, sir

be accusative affix

tuwanjiha Pret. (4) of *tuwanjimbi* to call (composed of *tuwambi* to see and *jimbi* to come)

jaide secondly

oci Cond. (6) of *ombi* to be

geli also

sakda old, experienced

ahun elder brother

de dative affix

baire Fut. Participle (5) of *baimbi* to request

babi from *ba* place, occasion and *bi* there is

damu but

baibi only

angga mouth

juwara Fut. Part. (5) of *juwambi* to open

de in

mangga difficult

ede so, then

aibi (from *ai* what and *bi* is) what?

gisun word, speech

bici Cond. (6) of *bimbi* to be: if there are words

uthai then

gisure Imp. (1) of *gisurembi* to speak

mini (gen. of *bi* I) my

mutere Fut. Part. (5) of *mutembi* to be able to do

baita matter

oci Cond. (6) of *ombi* to be

sinde dative of *si* thou

bi I

geli too

marimbio to turn the head away, to back out, with interrogative *o*.

So I am come to-day, sir, in the first place, to pay my respects to you, and, in the next, to ask a favour of you. I find it not so easy to open the subject, however.

SENIOR. What's your difficulty? pray say what you have got to say. If it's anything that I can do for you, do you suppose that, with the relations existing between us, I shall try to back out?

1	2	3	4

JUNIOR. What I have to ask, then, is this: that you will so far take an interest in me as to put yourself to a little trouble on my account; I will tell you how. Find time, if you can, to compose a few phrases in Manchu for me to study, and if I manage to succeed at all, I shall regard it entirely as your work.

mini my

bairengge Fut. Part. (21) of *baimbi* to request: that which I shall request

age elder brother, sir

gosici Cond. (6) of *gosimbi* to be kind to

šadambi Present (2) to be (get) tired

seme Inf. or Ger. (3) of *sembi* to say: saying

ainara Fut. (5) of *ainambi* to do what?

šolo leisure

šolo leisure

de in

udu several, some

meyen chapter

manju Manchu

gisun word, speech

banjibufi Past Ger. (8) of *banjibumbi* to create, prepare: having prepared

minde dat. for me

hūlabureo Future (5) of causative of *hūlambi* to read, to study with *o* implying a request: please cause me to study

deo younger brother

bi I

bahafi Past Ger. (8) of *bahambi* to obtain, to succeed

hūwašaci Cond. (6) of *hūwašambi* to increase, to prosper

gemu entirely

age elder brother, sir

i genitive affix

kesi grace

kai is (final particle).

1	2	3	4

Sir, I shall never forget your kindness, and shall not fail to repay it handsomely.

Senior. What are you talking about? you are one of us, are you not? My only fear would have been that you were not anxious to learn; but, since you are willing, I shall be only too glad to contribute to your success.

ainaha seme certainly

baili kindness

be accusative affix

onggorakū Fut. (5) of *onggombi* to forget, with *akū* not

urunakū must

ujeleme Ger. (3) of *ujelembi* to make heavy, to increase: increasingly

karulaki Subj. (7) of *karulambi* to repay

ainu why ?

uttu thus

gisurembi to speak

si thou

aika perhaps

gurun empire } foreigner, with interrogative *o*
gūwao other

damu only

sini gen. of *si* thou

tacirakū Fut. (5) of *tacimbi* to learn, with *akū* not.

be accusative affix

hendumbi to speak

dere final particle expressing a doubt

taciki Subj. (7) of *tacimbi* to learn

seci Cond. (6) of *sembi* to say, to be willing

tetendere supposing

bi I

nekulefi Past Ger. (8) of *nekulembi* to be useful

simbe acc. of *si* thou

niyalma man

okini Opt. (15) of *ombi* to make

sembikai to say, with *kai*, final particle

1	2	3

Talk of handsome return, indeed! people as intimate as you and I are should never use such language to one another.

JUNIOR. Well, sir, if that's the way of it, I am sure I feel extremely obliged. I have only to make you my best bow, and I shall say no more.

karulaki Subj. (7) of *karulambi* to repay

serengge Verbal Noun (21) of *sembi* to say: that which you said

ai what?

gisun word, speech

musei gen. of *muse* we, we two

dolo interior, in the family

gisureci Cond. (6) of *gisurembi* to speak

ombio to be, can, may, with interrogative *o*: will that do?

tuttu thus

oci Cond. (6) of *ombi* to be

bi I

hukšehe Pret. (4) of *hukšembi* to be thankful

seme Inf. or Ger. (3) of *sembi* to say

wajirakū Fut. (5) of *wajimbi* to end, with *akū* not: infinitely

damu only

hengkišeme Inf. or Ger. (3) of *hengkišembi* to prostrate oneself

baniha thanks

bure Fut. (5) of *bumbi* to give

dabala only

geli besides

ai what?

sere Fut. (5) of *sembi* to say.

21

1	2	3	4

II. SENIOR. Why, when did you find, time to learn all the Manchu you know sir? Your pronunciation is good and you speak quite intelligibly.

JUNIOR. Oh, sir, you are too complimentary. My Manchu does not amount to anything. There's a friend of mine who really does talk well;

age elder brother, sir
sini thy
manju Manchu
gisun word, speech
ai what ?
šolo leisure
de in
taciha Pret. (4) of *tacimbi* to learn
mudan pronunciation
gairengge Verbal Noun (21) of *gaimbi* to take, to obtain
sain good
bime Ger. (3) of *bimbi* to be
tomorhon clear
mini my
manju Manchu
gisun word, speech
be accusative affix
ai what ?
dabufi Past. Ger. (8) of *dabumbi* to count
gisurere Fut. Part. of *gisurembi* to speak
babi from *ba* place and *bi* it is
age elder brother, sir
gosime Ger. (3) of *gosimbi* to love
ofi Past Gerund (8) of *ombi* to be
uttu thus
dabali excessively
maktara Fut. (5) of *maktambi* to praise
mini my
emu one
gucu friend
i genitive affix
manju Manchu
gisun word, speech
sain good

1	2	3	4

getuken intelligible
bime Ger. (3) of *bimbi* to be
dacun quick, fluent
majige little
nikan Chinese
mudan pronunciation
akū not
umesi very
urehebi Indef. Past (10) of *urembi* to be
    ripe, proficient
tuttu thus
bime Ger. (3) of *bimbi* to be
šan ear
geli further
fe old, the meaning is: he has heard much
    old language
tere he
teni high, with adverbial affix *i*
mangga difficult, qualified
seci Cond. (6) of *sembi* to say, to call
ombi to be
tere he
sinci from *si* thou and *ci* from, to express
    the comparative
antaka how?
bi I
adarame how?
inde dat. of *i* he: to him
duibuleci Cond. (6) of *duilembi* to compare
ombini to be, with interrogative *ni*: would
    that do?
fuhali altogether
tede dat. of *tere* he
bakcin rival, match
waka not

He is thoroughly at home in the language—intelligible, fluent, and speaks without a particle of Chinese accent, he is quite proficient. Then, besides, he has such a stock of words and phrases. Now, that is what one may call a good scholar, if you please.

SENIOR. How does he compare with you?

JUNIOR. Me! I should never venture to compare myself with him; I am as far from being his match

1	2	3	4

abka heaven
na earth
i genitive affix
gese equal
sandalabuhabi Ind. Past. (10) of *sandala-bumbi* to be separated.
turgun reason
ai what?
seci Cond. (6) of *sembi* to say, call
ini his
tacihangge verbal noun (21) of *tacimbi* to learn
šumin deep
bahanahangge Verbal Noun (21) of *baha-nambi* to comprehend
labdu much
bithe book
de in, for
amuran having a passion for
tetele till now
hono also
angga mouth
ci from
hokoburakū Fut. (5) of *hokobumbi* to leave off, with *akū* not
hūlambi to read, study
gala hand
ci from
aljaburakū Fut. of *aljabumbi* to separate, with *akū* not
tuwambi to see, to look
imbe him
amcaki Subj. (7) of *amcambi* to reach
seci Cond. of *sembi* to say
yala certainly
mangga difficult

as the heavens are from the earth.

SENIOR. What is the reason of that?

JUNIOR. Oh, he has been much longer at it, and knows a great deal more. Then he is very studious; he has been committing to memory steadily ever since he began, without stopping; the book is never out of his hand. I should have trouble enough to come up to him.

1	2	3	4

(Manchu script, columns 1–4)

SENIOR. Nay, my young friend, I think you are making a slight mistake. Don't you remember what the proverb says: "If you are constant, you will penetrate a rock"? What he knows he knows only because he has learnt it; it has not come to him by intuition. And are we in any way otherwise constituted? not at all!

age elder brother, sir
sini thy
ere this
gisun word, speech
majige little
tašarabuhakū Pret. (4) of *tašarabumbi* to cause an error, with *akū* not
semeo Inf. or Ger. (3) of *sembi* to say, to think, with interrogative *o*
donjici Cond. (6) of *donjimbi* to hear
hing with *sembi* to be careful, constant
sere Fut. (5) of *sembi* to say
oci Cond. (6) of *ombi* to be: if
hada rock
de in
hafumbi to penetrate
sehebi Indef. Past (10) of *sembi* to say
tere he
inu yes, also
tacifi Past Ger. (8) of *tacimbi* to learn
bahanahangge Verbal Noun (21) of *bahanambi* to comprehend
dabala only
umai not at all
banjinjifi Past Ger. (8) of *banjinjimbi* to come into life
bahanahangge Verbal Noun (21) of *bahanambi* to comprehend
waka not
kai is, final particle
muse we (two)
tede dat. of *tere* he: to him
isirakūngge Verbal Noun (21) of *isimbi* to arrive, with *akū* not
ya whatsoever
ba place

1	2	3	4

(Manchu script in four columns)

i he

ai what?

hacin kind

i genitive affix

bahanaha Pret. (4) of *bahanambi* to comprehend

urehe Pret. (4) of *urembi* to be proficient

okini Opt. (15) of *ombi* to be, may

muse we

damu only

mujilen heart

be accusative affix

teng with *sembi* to be firm

seme Ger. (3) of *sembi* to say

jafafi Past Ger. (8) of *jafambi* to take

gūnin thought

girkūfi Past Ger. (8) of *girkūmbi* to exert

tacici Cond. (6) of *tacimbi* to learn

udu although

tere that

ten hight

de to, at

isiname Ger. (3) of *isinambi* to arrive

muterakū Fut. (5) of *mutembi* to be able, with *akū* not

bicibe Advers. (13) of *bimbi* to be

inu yes, certainly

urunakū without doubt

haminambi to come near

dere final particle expressing a presumption.

Well, then, no matter how exact or practised a speaker he may be, all we have to do is to make up our mind and apply ourselves to the language; and if we don't quite reach the point he has attained, we shall not be very far behind him, I suspect.

1	2	3	4

si thou

nikan Chinese

bithe book

bahanara Fut. Part. (5) of *bahanambi* to comprehend

niyalma man

kai is, final particle

ubaliyambure Fut. (5) of *ubaliyambumbi* to translate

be accusative affix

tacici Cond. (6) of *tacimbi* to learn

umesi very

ja easy

dabala only

gūnin thought

girkūfi Past Ger. (8) of *girkūmbi* to exert

giyalan interval

lakcan interruption

akū not

emu one; *emu anani* one after the other, without interruption

tacime Ger. (3) of *tacimbi* to learn

ohode supposing, if

juwe two

ilan three

aniya year

i genitive affix

siden middle

de in

III. SENIOR. As to becoming a translator of Manchu, you are a Chinese scholar, and you can have no difficulty in learning to translate. All you need is an exclusive devotion of your mind to the one subject. Don't let anything interfere with your studies, and let these be progressive; and in two or three years,

1	2	3	4
᠊᠊᠊	᠊᠊᠊	᠊᠊᠊	᠊᠊᠊

ini cisui as a matter of course
dube point, end, extreme
da beginning, *dube da* the very beginning
tucimbi to come out
aika if
emu one
inenggi day
fiyakiyara Fut. (5) of *fiyakiyambi* to glow
juwan ten
inenggi day
šahūrara Fut. (5) of *šahūrambi* to be cold
adali like, similar to
tacici Cond. (6) of *tacimbi* to learn
uthai then
orin twenty
aniya year
bithe book
hūlaha Pret. (4) of *hūlambi* to read, study
seme Ger. (3) of *sembi* to say
inu yes, truly
mangga difficult
kai is, final particle.

———

age elder brother, sir
mini my
ubaliyambuhangge Verbal Noun (21) of
    ubaliyambumbi to translate
be accusative affix
tuwafi Past Ger. (8) of *tuwambi* to look at
majige little
dasatarao Fut. (5) of *dasatambi* to correct,
    with *o* implying a request.

as a matter of course, you will be well on your way. If you glow for one day and are cold for ten days in your study, you may read for 20 years, but it will come to nothing.

IV. JUNIOR. Will you do me the favour to look over these translations, sir, and make a few corrections?

1	2	3	4

(Manchu script, four vertical columns)

sini thy

tacihangge Verbal Noun (21) of *tacimbi* to learn

labdu much

nonggibuha Pret. (4) of *nonggibumbi* to make progress

gisun word, speech

tome all

ijishūn proper

hergen letter

aname singly

tomorhon clear

majige little

cilcin fault

akū not

simneci Cond. (6) of *simnembi* to be examined

seferehei Past Part. (4) of *seferembi* to take in the hand, with *i*, which makes the word an adverb

bahambi to obtain.

---

ere this

mudan time

ubaliyambure Fut. Part. (5) of *ubaliyambumbi* to translate

be accusative affix

simnere Fut. Part. (5) of *simnembi* to be examined

de in

gebu name

alibuhao Pret. (4) of *alibumbi* to offer, with interrogative *o*

akūn or not?

simneci Cond. (6) of *simnembi* to be examined

oci Cond. (6) of *ombi* to be

esi certainly

sain good

oci Cond. (6) of *ombi* to be

SENIOR. Oh, come, you really have made very great progress; every sentence runs as it should; every letter is clear; I have not a fault to find. If you go up for your examination, success is in your own hands.

V. SENIOR. Have you returned yourself as a candidate at these examinations that are coming off now?

JUNIOR. I should be glad enough to stand,

1	2	3	4
ᠨᡳᠶᠠᠯᠮᠠ	ᠨᡳᠶᠠᠯᠮᠠ	ᠨᡳᠶᠠᠯᠮᠠ	ᠨᡳᠶᠠᠯᠮᠠ

but I am afraid that, being a B. A., I am not qualified.

SENIOR. What? when any bannerman can go up, do you mean to say that a man of your attainments would not be allowed to? Nonsense! why even the boys from public schools may stand;

damu only

bithei book, with gen. affix *i* (文 wên)

šusai B. A. (秀 才 hsiu t'sai)

ainahai how should it?

ombini to be, it will do, with interrogative particle *ni*

wei whose?

kooli custom

sini thy

gesengge similar

jakūn eight

gūsa banner

gemu all

simneci Cond. (6) of *simnembi* to be examined

ombime Ger. I (16) of *ombi* to be, may

sini thy

beye body, self

teile only

simneburakū Fut. Pass. (5) of *simnembi* to be examined, with *akū* not: will not be allowed to be examined

doro rule

bio is, with interrogative *o*

tere that

anggala not only

jurgangga public (義 *i*)

tacikūi school, with gen. affix. *i*

juse plural of *jui* son, child, scholar

gemu all

ojoro Fut. (5) of *ombi* to be, may

bade when

1	2	3	4

and if so, how should a B. A. not be qualified? my younger brother is now working as hard as he can at Manchu for the little time that remains before he has to go up. Don't you throw away the opportunity. Add your name to the list at once.

šusai B. A.

be accusative affix

ai what?

hendure Fut. (5) of *hendumbi* to speak

simneci Cond. (6) of *simnembi* to be examined

ome Inf. (3) of *ombi* to be, may

ofi Past Ger. (8) of *ombi* to be, because

mini my

deo younger brother

ere this

siden interval

de to, in

teni highly

hacihiyame Ger. (3) of *hacihiyambi* to exert oneself

manju Manchu

bithe book

hūlambikai to read, with *kai* final particle

hūdun quickly

gebu name

yabubu Imp. Pass. (1) of *yabumbi* to go: cause to go, forward

nashūn opportunity

be accusative affix

ume do not

ufarabure Fut. (5) of *ufarabumbi* to neglect.

1	2	3	4

sini thy

manjurarangge Verbal Noun (21) of *manjurambi* to speak Manchu

majige little

muru appearance

tucikebi Indef. Past (10) of *tucimbi* to
come forth

aibide how?

bi I

niyalmai man, with gen. affix *i*

gisurere Fut. Part. (5) of *gisurembi* to
speak

be accusative affix

ulhire Fut. (5) of *ulhimbi* to understand

gojime only

mini my

beye body, self

gisureme Ger. (3) of *gisurembi* to speak

ohode when

oron interval, place

unde not yet, *oron unde* not yet time, too
early

gūwai other, with gen. affix *i*

adali like, similar

fiyelen chapter, piece, *fiyelen fiyeleni* con-
nectedly

gisureme Inf. (3) of *gisurembi* to speak

muterakū Fut. (3) of *mutembi* to be able,
with *akū* not

sere Fut. (5) of *sembi* to say

anggala not only

emu one

siran continuation

i adverbial particle, *emu sirani* uninter-
ruptedly

duin four

sunja five

gisun word

VI. SENIOR. Well, I hear that you have made such way in Manchu, that you are beginning to speak it quite correctly.

JUNIOR. Nonsense! I understand it, certainly, when I hear it spoken, but it will be sometime yet before I can speak it myself. It is not only that I can't go right through with a piece of conversation of any length like other people, but I can't even string half a dozen sentences together.

1	2	3	4

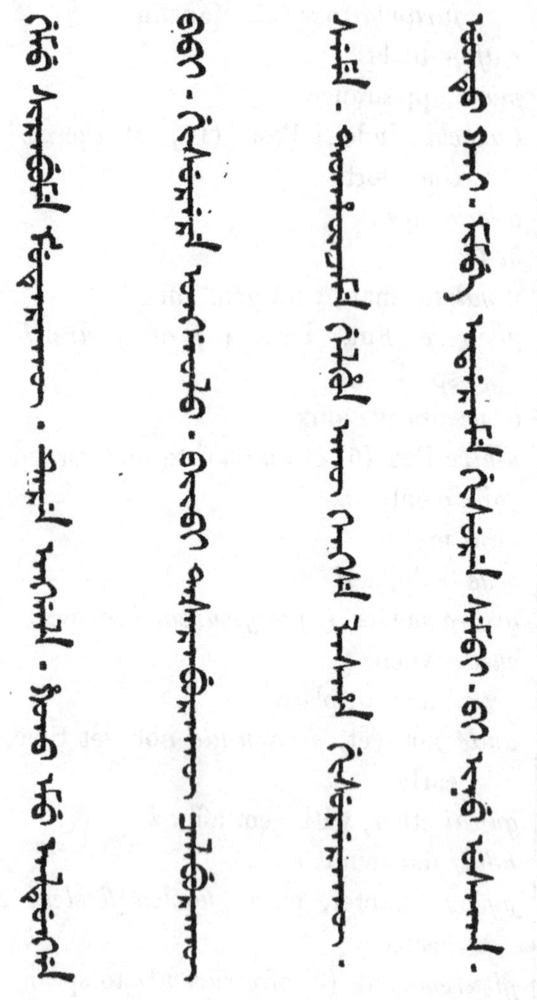

(Manchu script text in four vertical columns)

Then there is another odd thing I do: whenever I am going to begin, without being the least able to say why, I become so alarmed about mistakes that I dare not go on without hesitating; now, so long as this continues to be the case, how am I to make a speaker? Indeed, so far from considering myself one, I quite despair.

gemu all

sirabume Inf. (3) of *sirabumbi* to connect

muterakū Fut. (5) of *mutembi* to be able, with *akū* not

tere that

anggala not only

hono further

emu one

aldungga extraordinary, strange

babi place, with *bi* is

gisurere Fut. Part. (5) of *gisurembi* to speak

onggolo before

baibi in vain

tašaraburakū Fut. (5) of *tašarabumbi* to make mistakes, with *akū* not

calaburakū Fut. (5) of *calabumbi* to err, with *akū* not

seme Inf. (3) of *sembi* to say

tathūnjame Inf. (3) of *tathūnjambi* to doubt, to be incertain, to be alarmed

gelhun akū without fear, tô dare

kengse lasha constantly

gisurerakū Fut. (5) of *gisurembi* to speak, with *akū* not

uttu thus

kai it is

mimbe acc. of I

adarame how ?

gisure Imp. (1) of *gisurembi* to speak

sembi to say, to call

bi I

inu yes, indeed

usaka in despair.

1	2	3	4

of ever learning to speak. I say to myself that if with all my studying I have not got farther than this, I shall certainly never be a proficient.

SENIOR. This is all mere want of practice. Listen to me. Whenever you meet a man, no matter who, (that can talk Manchu), at him at once, and talk away with him.

gūnici Cond. (6) of *gūnimbi* to think
ai what?
hacin kind
i genitive affix
taciha Pret. (4) of *tacimbi* to learn
seme Inf. (3) of *sembi* to say
inu indeed
ere this
hūman ability
dabala only
nonggibure Fut. (5) of *nonggibumbi* to make progress
aibi how could?
ere this
gemu all
sini thy
urehekū Pret. (4) of *urembi* to practice, with *akū* not
haran reason
bi I
sinde dat. of *si* thou
tacibure Fut. (5) of *tacibumbi* to teach
yaya whoever
webe acc. of *we* who
seme Inf. (3) of *sembi* to say
ume not, do not
bodoro Fut. (5) of *bodombi* to consider
damu only
ucaraha Pret. (4) of *ucarambi* to meet
ucaraha Part. Pret. (4) of *ucarambi* to meet
be sign of accusative
tuwame Ger. (3) of *tuwambi* to try
amcatame Ger. (3) of *amcatambi* to address one against his will
gisure Fut. (5) of *gisurembi* to speak.

34

1	2	3	4

jai secondly

bithede book, with *de* in

šungke well read

sefu teacher (師傅 shih-fu)

be accusative affix

baifi Past Gerund (8) of *baimbi* to seek

bithe book

hūla Imp. (1) of *hūlambi* to read

manju Manchu

gisun word, speech

de in

mangga proficient

gucuse plur. of *gucu* friend

de in, with

adanafi Past Gerund (8) of *adanambi* to go to, to be together

gisure Fut. (5), here Imp. of *gisurembi* to speak

inenggidari daily

hūlaci Cond. (6) of *hūlambi* to read

gisun word, speech

ejembi to remember

erindari always

gisureci Cond. (6) of *gisurembi* to speak

ilenggu tongue

urembi to be accustomed

uttu thus

tacime Inf. (3) *tacimbi* to learn

ohode when

manggai scarcely

emu one

juwe two

You must go and take lessons of competent professors of the language as well, you know; and if you have any friends who are good Manchu scholars, you should be for ever talking with them. Read some Manchu every day, and talk incessantly, until the habit of speaking comes quite naturally to the mouth. If you follow this rule in a year or two at the farthest

1	2	3	4

aniya year

i genitive affix

sidende interval, with *de* in

inu yes, certainly ; *inu cisui* naturally

gūnin thought

i sign of genitive

cihai will, with adverbial affix *i*, *gūnin i cihai* as you like

anggai mouth, with genitive affix

ici in accordance

tang sembi to speak without interruption

kai final particle

muterakū Fut. (5) of *mutembi* to be able, with *akū* not

jalin as regards

geli again

aiseme how could it ?

jobombi to apprehend, to fear

ni interrogative particle.

---

absi why ?

yoha Pret. (4) of *yombi* to go, to walk

bihe Pret. (4) of *bimbi* to be

bi I

ergi this side

emu one

niyamangga related

niyalmai man, with genitive affix *i*

boode house, with *de* in

genehe Pret. (4) of *genembi* to go

bihe Pret. (4) of *bimbi* to be

ere this

ildun opportunity

de in

mini my

boode house, with *de* in, to

darifi Past Gerund (8) of *darimbi* to pass

majige little

teki Subj. Present (7) of *tembi* to sit down.

you will speak it without an effort; so now don't despair any more.

VII. JUNIOR. Where are you from, sir, may I ask ?

SENIOR. I have been to visit a relation of mine who lives down yonder. Won't you step in and sit down on your way, sir ?

1	2	3	4

age elder brother, sir

si thou

ubade here

tehebio Indef. Past. (10) of *tembi* to sit, to reside, with interrogative *o*

inu yes

jakan lately

gurinjihe Pret. (4) of *gurinjimbi* to come to change place

uttu thus

oci Cond. (6) of *ombi* to be

musei we two, with genitive affix *i*

tehengge Verbal Noun (21) of *tembi* to sit, to reside

giyanakū far from

udu how much?

goro distant

saha Pret. (4) of *sambi* to know

bici Cond. (6) of *bimbi* to be

aifini before

simbe acc. of *si* thou

tuwanjirakū Fut. (5) of *tuwanjimbi* to come to see, to call, with *akū* not

biheo Pret. (4) of *bimbi* to be, with interrogative *o*

age elder brother, sir

yabu Imp. (1) of *yambumbi* to go

ai geli how could that be?

mini my

boode house, with postpos. *de* in

kai it is

age elder brother, sir

wesifi Past Gerund (8) of *wesimbi* to ascend

teki Subj. Pres. (2) of *tembi* to sit

ubade here

icangga convenient

si thou

tuttu thus

tehede seat, with postpos. *de* in

bi I

absi how?

tembi to sit.

JUNIOR. Do you reside in this neighbourhood, sir?

SENIOR. Yes, I moved into this house not long ago.

JUNIOR. Oh! indeed, sir; then we are not so very far from each other. If I had been aware that you lived here, I should have called before. Go on, sir, pray (I'll follow you, if you please).

SENIOR. What, in my own house? Now, please take the upper seat.

JUNIOR. Thank you, I am very well where I am.

SENIOR. But if you sit where you are sitting, what place am I to take?

1	2	3	4

sain good
teme Inf. (3) of *tembi* to sit
jabduha Pret. (4) of *jabdumbi* to reach one's aim
ubade here
emu one
nikere Fut. Partic. (5) of *nikembi* to lean against
babi place (*ba*) is (*bi*)
booi house, with genitive affix *i*
urse those who
aba how?
yaha coal
gaju Imp. (1) of *gajimbi* to fetch
age elder brother, sir
bi I
dambagu tobacco
omirakū Fut. (5) of *omimbi* to eat, to smoke, with *akū* not
angga mouth
furugahabi to have ulcers in the mouth
tuttu thus
oci Cond. (6) of *ombi* to be
cai tea
gana Imp. (1) of *ganambi* to bring
age elder brother, sir
cai tea
gaisu Imp. (1) of *gaimbi* to take
ko oh, exclamation of pain
absi how?
halhūn hot
halhūn hot
oci Cond. (6) of *ombi* to be
majige little
tukiyecebu Imp. (1) of *tukiyecebumbi* to take away
hūwanggiyarakū it does not signify
mukiyebukini Opt. (15) of *mukiyebumbi* to become cool
je exclamation of compassion
buda rice
be accusative affix
tuwana Imp. (1) of *tuwanambi* to go and look after

JUNIOR. I have got a seat, thank you; and a seat with a back to it.

SENIOR. Here! bring a light!

JUNIOR. Not for me, thank you, sir, I can't smoke; I have a sore mouth.

SENIOR. Well, then, bring some tea.

JUNIOR. Drink first, then, pray. Oh, isn't it hot.

SENIOR. If it is too hot, let it be taken away for a while, that it may get cooler. I am very sorry. Boy, go and see what there is in the kitchen,

1	2	3	4

beleni ready
bisirengge Verbal Noun (21) of *bimbi* to be
be accusative affix
hasa quickly
banju Imp. (1) of *banjimbi* to produce
se Imp. (1) of *sembi* to say
akū no
age elder brother, sir
ume do not
bi I
kemuni further
gūwa other
bade place, with *de* to
geneki Subj. Pres. (7) of *genembi* to go
sembi to say
ainahabi how is that ?
beleni ready
bisirengge Verbal Noun (21) of *bimbi* to be
sini thy
jalin postpos. on account of
dagilahangge Verbal Noun (21) of *dagilambi*
　　　　to prepare
geli also
waka not is
majige little
jefi Past Ger. (8) of *jembi* to eat
genecina Concessive (14) of *genembi* to go
joo enough
bi it is
emgeri once
sini thy
boo house
be accusative affix
takaha Pret. (4) of *takambi* to recognise
kai it is
encu different, other
inenggi day
jai again
cohome specially
jifi Past. Ger. (8) of *jimbi* to come

and bring quickly whatever is ready.

JUNIOR. No, indeed, sir; do not put yourself to so much trouble. I have still got to go somewhere else.

SENIOR. But it's only whatever is ready; nothing is being prepared for you. Do try and eat a little, then you may go.

JUNIOR. Not just now, thank you, sir; but now that I have found out where you live, I'll come another time

1	2	3	4
ᠮᠠᠨᠵᡠ	ᠮᠠᠨᠵᡠ	ᠮᠠᠨᠵᡠ	ᠮᠠᠨᠵᡠ

gulhun completely

emu one

inenggi day

gisureme Inf. (3) of *gisurembi* to speak

teceki Subj. Pres. (7) of *tecembi* to sit together.

---

age elder brother, sir

si thou

inenggidari daily

ederi this way

yaburengge Verbal Noun (21) of *yabumbi* to go

gemu all

aibide whither?

genembi to go

bithe book

hūlaname Inf. (3) of *hūlanambi* to go to read

genembi to go

manju Manchu

bithe book

hūlambi to read

wakao it is not, with interrogative *o*

inu yes

ne now

aici which?

jergi order

bithe book

hūlambi to read

gūwa other

bithe book

akū not

damu only

yasai eye, with genitive affix *i*

juleri postpos. before

buyarame Ger. (3) of *buyarambi* to do petty things

gisun word, speech

and spend the day with you.

VIII. SENIOR. I observe you pass this way every day, sir, what place is it that you go to?

JUNIOR. I go to my studies.

SENIOR. To read Manchu, isn't it?

JUNIOR. It is.

SENIOR. What are you reading in Manchu?

JUNIOR. Oh, no new books, only every day talk

1	2	3	4

(Manchu script columns)

jai secondly
manchu Manchu
gisun word, speech
i genitive affix
oyonggo important
jorin aim, explanation
i genitive affix
bithe book
teile only
suwende dat. of *suwe* you
ginggulere Fut. Part. (5) of *ginggulembi* to honour; here with *hergen* the 楷書 ch'ieh-shu an elegant style of writing
hergen letter, writing
tacibumbio to teach, with interrogative *o*
akūn or not?
te now
inenggi day } day
šun sun
foholon short
hergen letter
arara Fut. Part. (5) of *arambi* to write
šolo leisure
akū not is
ereci this, with postpos. *ci* from, hereafter
inenggi day } day
šun sun
saniyaha Pret. (4) of *saniyambi* to extend
manggi as soon as
hergen letter
arabumbi Pass. of *arambi* to write; to cause to write
sere Fut. (5) of *sembi* to say
anggala not only
hono also
ubaliyambu Imp. (1) of *ubaliyambumbi* to translate
sembikai to say, with *kai* final particle
age elder brother, sir
bi I
bithe book
hūlara Fut. Part. (5) of *hūlambi* to read
jalin because of

and the "Important explanation of Manchu speech." *

SENIOR. Are they teaching you to write Manchu round hand yet?

JUNIOR. The days are too short at present to leave any time for writing; but presently, when they begin to lengthen, we shall be taught to write and to translate, too.

SENIOR. Well, sir, I have been wanting to study Manchu myself

* See Essay on Manchu Literature, page 10.

1	2	3	4

yala really
uju head
silgime Ger. (3) of *silgimbi* to put into
aibide where ?
baihanahakū Pret. (4) of *baihanumbi* to go
    to search, with *akū* not
musei we two, with genitive affix *i*
ubai here, with genitive affix *i*
šurdeme all round
fuhali altogether
manju Manchu
tacikū school
akū not
gūnici Cond. (6) of *gūnimbi* to think
sini thy
tacire Fut. Part. (5) of *tacimbi* to learn
ba place
ai what?
hendure Fut. (5) of *hendumbi* to speak
atanggi when ?   } whenever
bicibe Advers. (13) of *bimbi* to be } it may be
bi I
inu also
bithe book
hūlanaki Subj. Pres. (7) of *hūlanambi* to go
    to read
mini gen. of *bi* I
funde postpos. for
majige little
gisureci Cond. (6) of *gisurembi* to speak
ojoroo can, may, with interrogative *o*
age elder brother, sir
si thou
mende dat. plur. of *be* we
tacibure Fut. Part. (5) of *tacibumbi* to teach
niyalma man
be accusative affix
we who
sembi to say, call ;

and I have looked, I assure you, everywhere (for a school) and left no place unexamined ; but in our neighbourhood, I am sorry to say, there is no school for Manchu.

I was thinking that the one you go to would do for me well enough, and that one of these days I might commence my attendance. Will you be so good as to say a word for me to the master beforehand?

JUNIOR. Ah! I see you think that it is a regular professor that teaches us ; but that

1	2	3	4

sefu teacher (師傅 shih fu)
sembio to say, call, with interrogative *o*
waka no
kai final particle.
mini my
emu one
mukūn clan
i genitive affix
ahūn elder
tacibure Fut. Part. (5) of *tacibumbi* to teach
ele whoever
urse plural affix
gemu all
meni our
emu one
uksun relationship
i genitive affix
juse pl. of *jui* son
deote pl. of *deo* younger brother
jai secondly
niyaman blood relation
hūncihin relation by marriage
umai not at all
gūwa other
niyalma man ✓
akū not is
adarame how
seci Cond. (6) of *sembi* to say
mini my
ahūn elder
inenggidari daily
yamulambi to go to the yamên
jabdurakū Fut. (5) of *jabdumbi* to have leisure, with *akū* not
ineku the same
be accusative affix
erde morning
yamji evening
nandame Inf. (3) of *nandambi* to request
genere Fut. (5) of *genembi* to go
jakade conj. because
arga trick, expedient

is not the case. Our instructor is one of the elders of our clan and his pupils are all our own near cousins; any others that may attend are relations by marriage; there is not an outsider among them. But the fact is that our elder is too busy to give regular lessons; for, besides teaching us, he has to go to the yamên every day. It is only because we entreat him day and night

1	2	3	4

akū not, *arga akū* he cannot help it
šolo leisure
jalgiyanjafi Past Ger. (8) of *jalgiyanjambi* to supply
membe acc. of *be* we
tacibumbi to teach
waka not
oci if
age elder brother, sir
bithe book
hūlame Inf. (3) of *hūlambi* to read
geneki Subj. Pres. (7) of *genembi* to go
sehengge Verbal Noun (21) of *sembi* to say
sain good
baita thing
dabala only
sini gen. of *si* thou
funde postpos. for
majige little
gisureci Cond. (6) of *gisurembi* to speak
minde dat. of *bi* I
geli then
ai what
wajiha Pret. (4) of *wajimbi* to end, finish
ni interrogative particle.

―――――

tere that
age elder brother
serengge Verbal Noun (21) of *sembi* to say
musei our, with genitive affix *i*
fe old
adaki neighbour
kai is
kemneme Inf. (3) of *kemnembi* to measure ⎫ to regard
tuwame Inf. (3) of *tuwambi* to see ⎬ carefully
mutuha Pret. (4) of *mutumbi* to grow ⎭

that he feels obliged to find time to play the tutor. Were the case otherwise, your desire to study Manchu is a thing commendable in itself, and as for the trouble of speaking in your behalf, I should not have thought it any trouble at all.

IX. SENIOR. That gentleman is our old neighbour, you know; the lad we have seen grow up here.

1	2	3	4

juse plur. of *jui* child
kiyalafi Past Ger. (8) of *kiyalambi* to be separated
giyanakū how could
udu how much
goidaha Pret. (4) of *goidambi* to last
donjici Cond. (6) of *donjimbi* to hear
mujakū exceedingly
hūwašafi Past Ger. (8) of *hūwašambi* to increase, to get on
hafan official
oho Pret. (4) of *ombi* to be
sere Fut. (5) of *sembi* to say
sucungga first
bi I
hono also
akdara Fut. (5) of *akdambi* to believe
dulin half
kenehunjere Fut. (5) of *kenehunjembi* to doubt
dulin half
bihe Pret. (4) of *bimbi* to be
amala afterwards
gucuse pl. of *gucu* friend
de postpos. in
fonjici Cond. (6) of *fonjimbi* to ask
mujangga certain
erebe this, with accusative affix *be*
tuwaci Cond. (6) of *tuwambi* to see, to regard
mujin resolution
bisirengge Verbal Noun (21) of *bimbi* to be
baita thing
jiduji completely
mutebumbi it can be done
se year
mulan seat; *se mulan* age
de postpos. in
akū not
sehe Pret. (4) of *sembi* to say
gisun word
tašan wrong

He has not been away from us very long, and now one hears that he is doing very well; that he has got an appointment. I only half believed the report when I first heard it, until on inquiring of friends I find it really is the case. It shows the truth of the proverb "If a man but resolve, the thing he wants to do is done"; and of the other proverb "No man is too young to make a resolution."

1	2	3	4

akū not
ni final particle
age elder brother, sir
i genitive affix
gisun word
inu true
tuttu thus
secibe Advers. (13) of *sembi* to say
inu certainly
terei his
sakdasa pl. of *sakda* old man, father
de postpos. in
wajirakū infinite
sain good
ba place
bifi Past Ger. (5) of *bimbi* to be
teni therefore
ere this
gese similarity
dekjingge prosperous
juse child
banjiha Pret. (4) of *banjimbi* to beget
nomhon kind
bime Ger. (3) of *bimbi* to be
sain good
tacin learning
jorin interpretation
de postpos. in
amuran fond of
gabtara Fut. Part. (5) of *gabtambi* to shoot on foot (with the bow)
niyamniyara Fut. Part. (5) of *niyamniyara* to shoot on horseback
eiten every
haihai man, with sign of genitive *i*
erdemu virtue
se year, age
de postpos. to
teisu corresponding to
akū not
ambula greatly
tacihabi Indef. Past (10) of *tacimbi* to learn, to study
an i ucuri generally

JUNIOR. That is all very well, sir; still, his father's infinite virtues must have enabled him to beget a son of such promise; a young man so kind and good, so fond of his studies; in foot and horse archery, in every manly exercise beyond his years accomplished; spending any spare time

1	2	3	4

boode house. with postpos. *de* in
bici Cond. (6) of *bimbi* to be
bithe book
tuwara Fut. (5) of *tuwambi* to look at
dabala only
balai frivolous
bade place, with postpos. *de* to
emu one
okson step
seme Inf. (3) of *sembi* to say
inu really
feliyerakū Fut. (5) of *feliyembi* to walk, with *akū* not
tere that
anggala not only
siden public
i genitive affix
baita affair
de postpos. in
oci Cond. (6) of *ombi* to be
ginggun careful
olhoba attentive
bahara Fut. Part. (5) of *bahambi* to obtain
sara Fut. Part. (5) of *sambi* to know
bade place, with postpos. *de* in
oci Cond. (6) of *ombi* to be
fimenere Fut. Part. (5) of *fimenembi* to smudge
ba place
akū not is
ere this
tob right
seme Inf. (3) of *sembi* to say
sain good
ba place
iktambuha Part. Pret. (4) of *iktambumbi* to accumulate
boode house, with postpos. *de* in
urunakū must
funcetele superabundant
hūturi luck
bi has
sehe Pret. (4) of *sembi* to say
gisun word, speech
de postpos. in
acanaha Pret. (4) of *acanambi* to agree

at home, and there always at his studies; never moving one step in the direction of a dissolute life.

Then he is so careful and attentive in the discharge of his public duties; and when he is able to obtain information about something, he remains perfectly spotless. It is quite a case in which one may observe that "The house where virtue accumulates (from generation to generation) will not fail to have more than an ordinary share of happiness."

1	2	3	4

X. JUNIOR. Keep on your horse, sir, pray! I went out of your sight.

Now, why should you go through the form of dismounting when you are so tired?

SENIOR. Not dismount, indeed! If I had not seen you, well and good; but when I did see you ever so far off, you would not have had me pass you on horseback, would you?

JUNIOR. Well, sir, won't you step in and sit down?

SENIOR. Oh, yes, I'll step in and sit down a moment, it is so long since we met.

secina Concess. (14) of *sembi* to say

age elder brother, sir
yalu Imp. (1) of *yalumbi* to ride
bi I
sinde Dat. of *si* thou
jailaha Pret. (4) of *jailambi* to escape
kai final particle
šadame Ger. (3) of *šadambi* to be tired
geli also
aiseme how could
ebumbi to dismount
ai gisun what language
serengge Verbal Noun (21) of *sembi* to say
sabuhakū Pret. (4) of *sabumbi* to notice, with *akū* not
oci Cond. (6) of *ombi* to be
ainara what is to be done?
bi I
kejine far off
aldangga distant
ci postpos. from
uthai therefore
simbe acc. of *si* thou
sabuha Pret. (4) of *sabumbi* to notice
bade conj. because
morilahai Part. Pret. (4) of *morilambi* to ride, with adverbial affix *i*: on horseback
dulere Fut. Part. (5) of *dulembi* to pass
kooli custom
bio it is, with interrogative *o*
age elder brother, sir
boode house, with postpos. *de* in, to
dosifi Past Ger. (8) of *dosimbi* to enter
terakūn Fut. (5) of *tembi* to sit, with *akūn* or not?
inu yes
kai final particle
muse we two
acahakūngge Verbal Noun (21) of *acambi* to meet, with *akū* not
kejine far off.

1	2	3	4

But, dear me! what a show of trees and flow-
ers you have, and what a stock of goldfish!
and your rockery, so ingeniously conceived;
every tier of it has a character of its own!
and what a tidy library! everything in it
looks

goidaha Pret. (4) of *goidambi* to last
bi I
dosifi Past Ger. (8) of *dosimbi* to enter
majige little
teki Subj. Pres. (7) of *tembi* to sit
ara hallo!
utala so many
hacingga of all kinds
moo tree
ilha flower
tebuhebio Indef. Past (10) of *tebumbi* to
    plant, with interrogative *o*
geli also
utala so many
boconggo coloured } goldfish
nisiha small fish }
ujihebi Indef. Past (10) of *ujimbi* to nourish
wehe stone
ai what
jibsime Inf. (3) of *jibsimbi* to lay in tiers
iktambuhangge Verbal Noun (21) of *iktam-*
    bumbi, pass. of *iktambi* to heap up
inu really
sain good
gūnin thought
isinaha Part. Pret. (4) of *isinambi* to arrive
be accusative affix
umesi very
faksi ingenious
jergi order, tier, *jergi jergi* every tier
de postpos. in
gemu all
doro rule
yangse beauty
bi is, has
ere this
bithei book, with genitive affix *i*
boo house, room
yala certainly
bolgo clean
absi how
tuwaci Cond. (6) of *tuwambi* to regard

1	2	3	4

absi so
icangga fit, convenient
tob true
seme Ger. (3) of *sembi* to say
musei we, with genitive affix *i*
bithe book
hulaci Cond. (6) of *hūlambi* to read
acara Fut. Part. (5) of *acambi* to suit
ba place
damu but
korsorongge Verbal Noun (21) of *Korsombi* to be discontented
minde dat. of I
asuru many
gucu friend
gargan associate
akū not
emhun alone
bithe book
tacici Cond. (6) of *tacimbi* to learn
dembei extremely
simeli lonesome
ede this
ai what?
mangga difficult?
si thou
aika perhaps
eimerakū Fut. Pat. (5) of *eimembi* to be bored, with *akū* not
oci if
bi I
sinde dat. of *si* thou
gucu friend
arame Inf. (3) of *arambi* to represent
jici Cond. (6) of *jimbi* to come
antaka how
tuttu thus
oci Cond. (6) of *ombi* to be
minde dat. of *bi* I
tusa profit
oho Pret. (4) of *ombi* to be, to have
solinaci Cond. (6) of *solinambi* to go to invite

so convenient, it is quite the place for reading men like us.

JUNIOR. It is nice enough, no doubt; the misfortune is that I have no friend to study with, and studying all alone is tame work.

SENIOR. Well, there needn't be much difficulty on that score. I'll be your fellow-student, provided that I don't bore you; what say you?

JUNIOR. Bore, indeed! It will be a real blessing if you will. I never asked you

50

1   2

ᠶᠣᠩ ᡥᡝᠯᡝᠮᠪᡳ ᡳᠨᡴ ᡥᠣᠯᠣᠮᠪᠣᠰᡳ ᡴᡝ ᡝᠯᡳ ᠵᡳᡴᡳ ᡩᠣᡥᠣᠮᠪᡳ

ᡳᠨᠴᡳᠩᡝᠰ ᡤᠠᡩᠠ ᡝᠯᡴᡳ ᡥᠣᡩᠣᡳᠪᠣ ᠪᡳᠵᡳᡳ ᠸᠣᠩ

hono yet

jiderakū Fut. (5) of *jimbi* to come, with *akū* not

jalin postpos. on account of

jobošombikai to be uneasy, with *kai* final particle

yala indeed

jici Cond. (6) of *jimbi* to come

mini my

jabšan luck

dabala only

eimembi to be bored

sere Fut. (5) of *sembi* to speak

doro rule, custom

geli still

bio it is, with interrogative *o*.

to come, because I feared you would refuse; but if you really are coming I shall be the most fortunate of men.

INDEX of AFFIXES and TERMS.

(The number in brackets indicates the verbal affix as explained on page 9).

APPENDIX.

For Manchu Literature see my Essay on Manchu Literature in Journal of China Branch of R. A. S., Shanghai, vol. xxiv (1890) p. 1-45.

The following are the principal European works for the study of Manchu :—

J. KLAPROTH, Chrestomathie mandchou or recueil de textes mandchou. Paris, 1828. 8vo, 273 pp.

H. C. von der GABELENTZ, Elémens de la grammaire mandchone. Altenbourg, 1832. 8vo, 156 pp.

Additional remarks on the Manchu verb in "Beiträge zur mandschuischen Conjugations-lehre, Zeitschr. der D. M. Ges. xviii, p. 202-219.

—Sse-schu, Schu-king, Schi-king in mandschuischer Uebersetzung mit einem mandschu-deutschem Wörterbuch. Leipzig, 1864. 2 vols. 8vo.

Vol. I containing the romanized Manchu text of the four books (四書), the Shuking and Shiking. 304 pp.

Vol. II containing the dictionary, 231 pp.

T. T. MEADOWS, Translations from the Manchu language with the original text. Canton, 1849. 8vo.

A. WYLIE, T'sing-wen-k'i-mung, a Chinese grammar of the Manchu Tartar language with introductory notes on Manchu literature. Shanghai, 1855. 8vo, ii, lxxx, 310 pp.

F. KAULEN, Linguae mandschuricae institutiones quas conscripsit indicibus ornavit chres-tomathia et vocabulario auxit. Ratisbonae, 1856. 8vo., 152 pp.

W. WASSILYEFF, Manchu Chrestomathy. St. Petersburg, 1863. 8vo, 228 pp.

L. ADAM, Grammaire de la langue mandchou. Paris, 1873. 8vo, 137 pp.

SAKHAROFF, Complete Manchu-Russian Lexicon. St. Petersburg, 1875. Imp. 8vo, xxx, 1,636 pp.

G. von der GABELENTZ, Thai-kih-thu. Tafel des Urprinzips, chinesisch mit mandschuischer und deutscher Uebersetzung. Dresden, 1876. 8vo.

W. GRUBE, T'ung-schu des Ceu-tsi, chinesisch und mandschuisch mit Uebersetzung und Com-mentar. Wien, 1880. 8vo.

E. TEZA, Mangiurica, note raccolte. Pisa.

G. HOFFMANN, Grammatica mancese compendiata dall' opera zinese Zing wen ki mung. Turin, 1883. 8vo, 36 pp.

L. NOCENTINI, Il santo editto di Kanghi e l'amplificazione di Yung-ceng. Versione mancese. Firenze, 1883.

C. DE HARLEZ, Manuel de la langue mandchoue. Grammaire, anthologie et lexique. Paris, 1884. 8vo., 232 pp.

For older works see Manual of Chinese Bibliography by myself and my brother. Shanghai, 1876, p. 300-305.

Made in the USA
Monee, IL
18 March 2024